Items should be returned on or before the last date
shown below. Items not already requested by other
borrowers may be renewed in person, in writing or by
telephone. To renew, please quote the number on the
barcode label. To renew online a PIN is required.
This can be requested at your local library.
Renew online @ **www.dublincitypubliclibraries.ie**
Fines charged for overdue items will include postage
incurred in recovery. Damage to or loss of items will
be charged to the borrower.

Leabharlanna Poiblí Chathair Bhaile Átha Cliath
Dublin City Public Libraries

Dublin City
Baile Átha Cliath

Date Due	Date Due	Date Due
14. AUG 08.		
28. JAN 12		
20. MAR 14.		

HOLOCAUST

HOLOCAUST

SIMON ADAMS

FRANKLIN WATTS

LONDON•SYDNEY

Designer Jason Billin
Editor Jennifer Schofield
Art Director Jonathan Hair
Editor-in-Chief John C. Miles
Picture research Diana Morris

© 2005 Franklin Watts

First published in 2005
by Franklin Watts
96 Leonard Street
London
EC2A 4XD

Franklin Watts Australia
Level 17/207 Kent Street
Sydney NSW 2000

ISBN 0 7496 6357 X

A CIP catalogue record for this book
is available from the British Library.

Printed in China

Dewey number: 940.53'18

Note to parents and teachers:
Every effort has been made by the Publishers
to ensure that the websites in this book are
suitable for children, that they are of the
highest educational value, and that they
contain no inappropriate or offensive
material. However, because of the nature of
the Internet, it is impossible to guarantee
that the contents of these sites will not be
altered. We strongly advise that Internet
access is supervised by a responsible adult.

CONTENTS

Introduction

Only just over 60 years ago, one of the most terrible events in human history occurred in Europe. Millions of people were deliberately killed simply because they were Jews. Today we call this event the Holocaust.

"For evil to triumph, it is only necessary for good men to do nothing."

Edmund Burke (1729–97), English politician and philosopher

Murder on an industrial scale – a stockpile of shoes taken from prisoners at Auschwitz death camp.

The Death Toll

The Holocaust began in 1933 when the extreme Nazi Party, led by Adolf Hitler, came to power in Germany. By 1945, the Nazis had killed more than six million Jews in the worst act of mass murder or genocide in human history. The Nazis also killed another five million people including Roma and Sinti (travellers), mentally or physically disabled people, homosexuals, communists, trade unionists, Jehovah's Witnesses, Poles, Russians, and other opponents of the Nazi regime.

This book looks at the history of this appalling event, what caused it, and why and how it happened. It follows the development of the Holocaust from its origins in European anti-Semitism – prejudice against Jewish people – through the introduction of the first anti-Jewish laws in Germany in 1933 to the establishment of Jewish ghettos in major European cities after 1939. It then details the "final solution", the construction of the concentration and death camps in the early 1940s.

The Holocaust came to an end in 1945, when Nazi Germany was defeated at the end of World War Two by the allied armies of the USA, USSR, and Britain. By then, more than half the Jewish population of Europe – one-third of all Jews in the world – were dead.

Why We Remember

The Holocaust was not the first act of genocide in human history, nor will it be the last. The mass murder of the Armenians by the Turks in 1915 and of Hutus and Tutsis in Rwanda in 1994 both took place in the 20th century, but the scale of the Holocaust makes it unique.

Indeed, the very extent of the Holocaust is so staggering that it is difficult for us to understand it today. After the war, many of those who escaped death were unable to talk about it. Those that did talk were often not believed. It was not until the 1960s that the Holocaust began to be talked and written about and studied in any detailed way. Today we remember the Holocaust as one of the most evil events in history and the worst single atrocity of the 20th century. But we also remember it as a lesson from history that we must never forget.

Holocaust Words

The Holocaust: The name used since World War Two to describe the murder of more than six million Jews by the Nazis. The word holocaust comes from the Greek words *holo* (whole) and *kaustos* (from *kaiein*, to burn), and means "a sacrifice that is completely consumed by fire".

Shoah: The Hebrew term for the Holocaust, used in Israel and by Jews around the world.

Endlösung: German word meaning "final solution"; the Nazis used the phrase "final solution to the Jewish problem" when referring to the extermination of all Jews in Europe.

Genocide: The deliberate destruction of a racial, religious, political or ethnic group.

Anti-Semitism

The Holocaust did not suddenly begin in 1933, but had its roots deep in history. For centuries, anti-Semitism was common among otherwise civilised and Christian people.

Naming the Evil

The term "anti-Semitism" was first used by the German journalist Wilhelm Marr in 1873 in his pamphlet "Der Sieg des Judentums über das Germanentum" (The Victory of Judaism over Germandom). Like many other Germans, including the composer Richard Wagner, Marr believed that Jews were a threat to German society and prosperity.

In 1881, 225,000 Germans signed a petition to the German chancellor, Otto von Bismarck, calling for the "liberation" of the German people from Jewish domination. Many Germans objected to this anti-Semitism and anti-Semitic parties gained only 4 per cent of the vote in elections held in 1898. By 1907, however, they had 16 deputies in the *Reichstag* (German parliament).

History of the Jews

The Jews originally came from the area we now know as Israel and Palestine at the eastern end of the Mediterranean. In 63 BCE, the Romans conquered the Jewish kingdom of Judea. The Jews did not like their new masters, and rebelled against Roman rule in 66 CE and again in 132 CE. Both times they were heavily defeated. Many Jews then fled into exile and settled elsewhere in the Roman Empire, in North Africa and Europe.

Although the Jews worshipped a different god from the Romans, their religion was largely tolerated. But as Christianity spread throughout the Roman Empire, the Jews were attacked as the people who had killed Jesus Christ. Christians distrusted and disliked the Jews, and even spread rumours about them sacrificing Christian children.

The Rise of Anti-Semitism

The first massacres of Jews by Christians began in the late 11th century as French and English Crusaders, setting out to reconquer the Holy Land of Palestine from its Muslim rulers, killed thousands of Jews who had settled along the banks of the Rhine in Germany. Jews were later expelled from England, France, Germany and Spain. Massacres of Jews took place during each expulsion. Many Jews then settled in the relatively unpopulated and poor areas of Poland, Ukraine, and western Russia, although here too they were massacred.

Anti-Semitic propaganda was heavily used to reinforce prejudices and mistrust. This poster comes from 1930s Germany and states "The Eternal Jew". It portrays Jews as obsessed with money and in league with communists.

During the 19th century, conditions for Jews began to improve throughout western Europe as governments granted them political and religious freedom. Jews could now participate in commerce, government, industry, medicine and the arts. Many became rich, but this in turn bred a new prejudice against them. Jews were now attacked because they were successful.

In eastern Europe, however, most Jews lived in ghettos and continued to be persecuted. In Russia, the assassination of Tsar Alexander II in 1881 sparked a wave of pogroms (persecutions). Two million Jews fled to the USA, while 300,000 settled in Canada, Argentina, Britain, South Africa and elsewhere.

Anti-Semitism

66–73, 132–135 CE Unsuccessful revolts against Roman rule in Judea sends many Jews into exile in Europe.

1096 English and French Crusaders massacre German Jews during First Crusade.

1215 Roman Catholic Church forces Jews in Europe to wear distinctive clothes or badges.

1290 Jews expelled from England.

1306 Jews expelled from France.

1348 Jews blamed for causing the Black Death that kills one-third of Europe's population; many Jews subsequently killed in massacres.

1450–1520 Jews expelled from many German towns.

1492 Jews expelled from Spain.

1648 Massacres of Jews in Poland and Ukraine.

1790–91 Jews granted equal rights in France during French Revolution.

1848 Jews granted equal rights in Germany.

1858 Jews granted equal rights in Britain.

1873 Term "anti-Semitism" first appears in Germany.

1881 Assassination of Tsar Alexander II in Russia leads to numerous pogroms in Russia; 2.3 million Jews emigrate to USA and elsewhere.

The Nazis Come to Power

In 1918 Germany was forced to ask for peace at the end of World War One. The country was exhausted and close to revolution. Fifteen years later, an anti-Semitic political party took power promising to restore German greatness at the expense of Jewish lives.

Mein Kampf

Hitler spelt out his beliefs in his book *Mein Kampf* (My Struggle) which he wrote in prison. In it he stated that the Aryans – as he called blond-haired northern Europeans such as the Germans – were engaged in a permanent struggle with the Jews.

He believed the Jews wanted to destroy the purity of the Aryan race and dominate the world by taking over its political and economic institutions. The only way the German race could survive was to defeat and kill the Jews and expand the German homeland eastwards to give the Germans *lebensraum* (living room).

Treaty of Versailles

In 1914 Germany and its ally Austria-Hungary went to war against Britain, France and Russia at the start of World War One. The war came to an end in November 1918 when Germany was forced to ask for an armistice. Its troops were exhausted, military supplies had run low, food shortages were common, and revolution was breaking out in several cities.

The peace treaty agreed at Versailles in France in June 1919 was very harsh on Germany. Many Germans believed the reason their country had been forced to accept the humiliating terms was because it had been "stabbed in the back" or betrayed by enemies of the state, such as Jews and communists. Many extreme political parties sprung up to exploit this discontent, notably the National Socialist German Worker's Party – the Nazis – led by Adolf Hitler.

The Rise of the Nazis

Adolf Hitler (1889–1945) was born in Austria and served in the German army during World War One. After the war, he joined the extreme German Worker's Party and quickly made a name for himself as a political organiser and powerful public speaker. He soon took control of the renamed Nazi Party and built up its strength. At first he tried to seize power by force, but failed and was sent to prison.

After this setback, Hitler concentrated on taking power by legal means. He set up groups such as the

Hitler Youth to attract new members to the party, and exploited every grievance against the government in order to increase support. This tactic paid off after 1929 when the German economy collapsed during the worldwide economic slump. Industries failed and six million Germans were unemployed in the winter of 1931–32.

Taking Over

In 1930, the Nazis got 6.5 million votes (18 per cent of the total), rising to more than 13 million (37 per cent) in 1932. Party membership rose to two million in February 1933. By now Germany was ungovernable without the Nazis, but Hitler refused to share power unless he was made chancellor (prime minister). On 30 January 1933, President Hindenburg asked Hitler to form a new government. The Nazis were in power.

Nazis relied on elaborate ceremonies and parades to build up their power. This rally took place at Nuremberg in 1933.

1918–1933

Nov 1918 Germany accepts armistice to end World War One.

Jan 1919 German Worker's Party (DAP) formed in Munich.

June Germany accepts punitive peace terms at Versailles, France.

July German Weimar republic established.

Sept Hitler joins DAP.

Feb 1920 DAP renames itself National Socialist German Worker's Party (NSDAP), soon known as the Nazi Party.

July 1921 Hitler takes full control of the Nazi Party.

Nov 1923 Hitler attempts to seize power, but is arrested and sentenced to five years in prison; he serves nine months.

July 1925 Hitler publishes *Mein Kampf*, (see panel) his personal manifesto.

July 1926 Hitler Youth and other party organisations set up.

Oct 1929 Shares crash in New York, starting a worldwide economic slump.

April 1932 Hitler comes second in presidential election with 13.4 million votes (36 per cent).

July Nazis take 37% of the popular vote in the general election.

Jan 1933 Hitler forms Nazi government.

Kristallnacht

The Nazis took action against the Jews as soon as they came to power in 1933. From then on, daily life for Jews in Germany became more and more difficult.

The Nuremberg Laws

The Nuremberg Laws of September 1935 stripped Jews of their German citizenship and forbade them to marry Germans. Sex between Jews and non-Jews was strictly forbidden.

The laws defined as a Jew anyone who had three or more Jewish grandparents, or who had two Jewish grandparents and attended a synagogue. Anyone who married a Jew after the laws came into force and any children of such a marriage were also classified as Jewish.

The laws also spelt out how to treat *Mischlinge* (part Jews) of the first degree (half-Jews) and second degree (quarter-Jews). The effect of these laws was to extend Jewishness from a religious to a racial description, and to make all Jews subjects, not citizens, of Germany.

Total Power

Within days of seizing power, Hitler banned opposition parties and became a dictator. He set up the Gestapo, or secret police, with powers to arrest and imprison anyone considered to be an enemy of the state. The first concentration camp, at Dachau outside Munich, was built to hold these political prisoners – gypsies (Roma), criminals, homosexuals, Jews and other opponents. Here, and in other camps, the inmates were treated as slaves and often worked to death. In August 1934, Hitler became *Führer* (leader) following the death of President Hindenburg.

Attacking the Jews

The Nazis moved quickly against the Jews. Gangs of Nazi stormtroopers attacked and killed Jews, looted their shops and businesses, and burned their synagogues. A one-day boycott of Jewish businesses was organised for 1 April 1933, while the books of Jewish and other authors were publicly burned in Berlin University Square. Jews were fired from the civil service, judiciary, schools and universities, while Jewish actors and musicians could not perform.

Further measures were taken in 1935 to remove Jews and other non-Aryans from the armed services. This hit some Jews very hard, for they had fought bravely for their country during World War One but were now considered to be its enemies. Most importantly, the Nuremberg Laws stripped Jews of their citizenship and forbade marriages between Jews and Germans. The following year, all remaining

*This early colour photograph shows a synagogue
ablaze on Kristallnacht, 9-10 November 1938.*

Jewish businesses were "Aryanised", that is
transferred to German ownership with almost
no compensation.

Kristallnacht

Attacks against Jews came to a head in November
1938. Hirschel Grynszpan, a German Jew studying
in Paris, protested against the expulsion of his
parents to Poland by walking into the German
embassy and shooting a German official, who later
died. The result was an attack on 7,500 Jewish
shops, leaving the streets littered with glass, hence
the name of this pogrom – *Kristallnacht* (the night
of broken glass). Synagogues were burned or
smashed up and gravestones destroyed. Ninety-
one Jews were killed, 8,000 were expelled from
Berlin and about 35,000 – one in ten German Jews
– were rounded up and held for some months in
concentration camps. The future was now very
bleak for Jews in Germany.

1933–1938

Jan 1933 Hitler becomes chancellor (prime
minister) of Germany.

Feb Reichstag, or parliament building,
catches fire; Hitler uses this as an excuse
to ban opposition parties.

March Enabling Act gives Hitler dictatorial
powers.

March First concentration camp built at
Dachau; others soon built at
Sachsenhausen, Sachsenburg, Esterwegen
and, in 1937, Buchenwald.

1 April One-day boycott of Jewish businesses
organised.

April Gestapo secret police established.

May Books by Jewish and other authors
disliked by the Nazis burned in Berlin.

July Law for the Prevention of Offspring
with Hereditary Diseases legalises forced
sterilisation of people with epilepsy,
schizophrenia and other illnesses and
disabilities.

1 Aug 1934 President Hindenburg dies; Hitler
becomes Führer and supreme commander.

May 1935 Defence Law removes Jews and
other non-Aryans from the armed services.

Sept Nuremberg Laws strip Jews of their
citizenship.

9–10 Nov 1938 Kristallnacht attacks on Jews,
their homes, businesses and synagogues.

Ways of Escape

After the events of Kristallnacht, life in Germany became intolerable for the Jews. They had three main options, but each presented them with huge problems.

Palestine

During World War One, Britain stated that it would "view with favour the establishment in Palestine of a national home for the Jewish people". It did this in order to gain Jewish support in the war against Germany.

After the war, Britain received a mandate over Palestine. Thousands of Jews moved to Palestine to double its existing Jewish population in ten years. However, Palestine was already home to the Palestinian Arabs, who resented the new immigrants.

Britain tried to restrict Jewish immigration in order to pacify the Palestinians, but rioting broke out between the two communities in 1929–30 and an Arab revolt erupted in 1936. Despite this, Palestine became one of the few places where Jews could safely flee to escape Nazi oppression.

Fight or Stay?

The first option for Germany's Jews was to fight back in order to stop the Nazis carrying out their murderous attacks. But the Nazis had used the attack by a Jew on an embassy official in Paris as an excuse for Kristallnacht, and would always react to any resistance by the Jews with extreme violence.

The second option was to stay put and hope that Hitler would soon be overthrown and life would return to normal. Many German Jews had been

Half of Germany's Jewish pre-war population managed to flee by 1939. Here, Jews arrive in Britain to start new lives.

citizens of the country for generations and had fought bravely for Germany in World War One. It was their country, too, but Kristallnacht convinced many that this was no longer the case.

Emigration

The third option was to leave Germany. The Nazi government encouraged Jews to emigrate, but took their possessions and money, so they left with nothing but a suitcase of clothes. Other countries then refused to accept them because they were poor. As the numbers of Jews wanting to leave Germany increased, representatives of 32 countries met at Evian in France in July 1938 to discuss this issue. Only the Netherlands and Denmark agreed to accept more Jews. Most agreed with the Australian representative – "since we have no racial problems, we are not desirous of importing one" – and refused to help.

Helping the Jews to Flee

In Britain, Jewish charities arranged for Jewish children to travel to Britain and live with adoptive families. The first *Kindertransport* arrived in December 1938. From then on, two transports a week brought 9,354 children to safety; the last train left Berlin on 31 August 1939, the day before Germany invaded Poland, starting World War Two.

Other Jews managed to escape, including more than 100,000 to the USA and 63,500 to Argentina. In total, half the 500,000 Jews living in Germany in 1933 had fled abroad by 1939. Many of these Jews went to countries such as Poland, Hungary, France and the Netherlands, all soon to be occupied by Germany. Those German Jews who remained now faced a very bleak future.

1917–1939

Nov 1917 The Balfour Declaration: British foreign secretary Arthur Balfour promises Jews a homeland in Palestine.

April 1920 Britain receives mandate over Palestine from League of Nations.

1921, 1924 USA severely limits Jewish immigration, forcing Jews to look elsewhere for safety.

1925 Britain limits Jewish immigration into Palestine.

1929–30 Palestinian Arabs riot against Jewish immigration.

1934 Jewish groups organise illegal immigration into Palestine.

1936–39 Arab revolt against British rule in Palestine; fights also occur between Jews and Arabs while extremist Jewish groups attack British troops in protest at entry restrictions, and organise illegal immigration into Palestine.

March 1938 183,000 more Jews come under German rule as Germany takes over Austria.

July Evian Conference fails to assist Jewish emigration from Germany.

Oct Germany takes over Sudeten region of Czechoslovakia; 20,000 Jews flee into the rest of the unoccupied country.

Dec First Kindertransport of Jewish children arrives at Harwich, Britain.

March 1939 German troops occupy rest of Czechoslovakia; 57,000 Jews trapped in Prague.

Sept Half of Germany's half-million Jewish population has fled the country by the start of World War Two.

Invasion and Occupation

In September 1939, Germany invaded Poland, causing Britain and France to declare war. World War Two had begun. Within a year, German forces overran most of Europe, and millions of Jews came under Nazi rule.

Stars and Triangles

After the German invasion of Poland, all Jews over the age of 12 had to wear a white armband with a blue six-pointed Star of David. Jews living in those parts of Poland absorbed into Germany had to sew a yellow Star of David onto their clothes and were shot or imprisoned if they did not comply. By 1944, Jews across occupied Europe all wore the yellow star.

Homosexuals imprisoned by the Nazis had to wear a pink triangle, while the Roma wore a black triangle; other prisoners had different-coloured stars or triangles. Today these are symbols of resistance and pride, not shame.

The Fate of Poland's Jews

The invasion of Poland brought two million Jews under Nazi rule; 250,000 more managed to flee to safety in the USSR. As they occupied the country, German troops immediately killed 5,000 Jews and drove 34,000 more out of their homes and forced them to swim across the rivers along the border with Soviet-held eastern Poland. A special task force, known as the *Einsatzgruppen* (action groups), rounded up Jews from the countryside and herded them into ghettos in the main towns (see pages 18–19). Here they were joined by Jews expelled from Germany, Austria and Bohemia.

Thousands more Jews were sent to labour camps, many of them along the Soviet border, where they built fortifications and dug trenches. Councils of Jewish elders were set up to count the Jews in their area and supply Jewish reinforcements to the camps to replace those who had died of starvation or maltreatment. Many more Jews were shipped to these camps from Slovakia, an ally of Germany.

Western Europe

In April 1940, German troops invaded Denmark and Norway, bringing 9,100 Jews under Nazi rule. The following month, German troops invaded the Low Countries and France, bringing another 500,000 Jews under Nazi rule. A further 150,000 Jews were added to the total after Yugoslavia and Greece were occupied the following year.

German troops round up Jews in Warsaw, Poland, 1943.

Muddled Plans

Such large numbers of Jews presented the Nazis with a great problem because their policy towards the Jews was muddled. German Jews could still emigrate if they could find a country that would take them, but this was now almost impossible as Britain and its worldwide empire was at war with Germany and its borders were closed. Thousands of Jews were therefore deported into France, or eastwards into the "Lublinland reservation" set up south of Warsaw. Here the Nazis proposed to resettle all Jews under its control. However, the local authorities objected to the area becoming a Jewish dumping ground and the plan was abandoned. Another plan to send all Jews to the French island colony of Madagascar in the Indian Ocean collapsed because it was impossible to achieve during wartime.

1939–1941

Aug 1939 Germany and USSR agree non-aggression pact: Germany free to invade Poland without fear of Soviet attack; Poland to be divided between the two countries.

Sept Germany invades and occupies western Poland; USSR occupies eastern Poland; Britain and France declare war.

Oct First Jewish ghetto created in Poland.

Oct–Nov 250,000 Polish Jews escape across border into Soviet-held Poland, 20,000 flee south into Hungary and Romania; 34,000 expelled across the Soviet border, many of whom are killed.

Dec Two years' forced labour made compulsory for all Polish Jewish males aged 14–60; 127 labour camps set up by January 1940.

April 1940 Germany invades Denmark and Norway.

April 95,000 Jews penned into "Lublinland reservation" in southern Poland.

May Germany invades the Low Countries – Netherlands, Belgium, Luxembourg – and France; Britain fights on alone.

May Plan proposed to expel all European Jews to Madagascar in Indian Ocean.

Dec About 100,000 Jews killed in Poland since German invasion.

April 1941 Germany invades Yugoslavia and Greece.

> 66 *The ultimate aim of German foreign policy is the emigration of all Jews living in German territory.* 99

German foreign ministry statement, 25 January 1939

T4

In September 1939, Hitler ordered "programme T4", the first large-scale killing programme organised by the Nazis. Up to 70,000 mentally or physically disabled people were killed by lethal injection or poisoned with carbon monoxide gas pumped into sealed rooms disguised as showers. Their bodies were then burned in crematoria.

Later, a further 5,000 children were killed, as were many disabled Poles, prisoners of war and foreign workers. In total, more than 170,000 people considered to be "unworthy of life" were killed in the various "euthanasia programmes", as they were called. This programme was a rehearsal for the much larger programme of murdering all Jews.

Life in the Ghettos

Polish Jews, who had not been killed during the German invasion or managed to escape across the border, were rounded up and sent to ghettos (restricted areas) in the major towns. Here life was reduced to hell on earth.

Walled in

The first ghetto was established in Piotrkow, southwest of Warsaw, in October 1939. A further 22 ghettos were set up by December 1940. Some of these were in the existing Jewish areas, but most were in poor or neglected areas well away from city centres. The ghettos were walled or fenced in to stop people from escaping, and were massively overcrowded. Food and medical supplies were restricted, leading to hunger and disease.

The Warsaw Ghetto

The largest ghetto in Poland was set up in Warsaw. The area was already home to 280,000 Jews, but a further 192,000 were moved in from elsewhere. Food was strictly rationed: Germans living in Warsaw were entitled to 2,310 calories a day, Poles to 934, but Jews to only 183 calories, for which they had to pay nearly 20 times as much per calorie as Germans. Not surprisingly, thousands died of starvation and disease. A Jewish Council appointed by the Germans organised cultural and education activities and looked after the many orphans.

The face of a young Jewish girl in the Warsaw ghetto tells a story of sadness and fear.

Rounded up and herded like cattle, Jewish men, women and children are cleared from the ghettos and sent to the camps.

Resistance

After March 1942, the Germans began to remove Jews from the ghettos for "resettlement" – that is murder (see pages 20–23), but resistance groups sprang up to resist deportations.

In the Warsaw ghetto, Jewish youths formed the Jewish Combat Organisation and armed themselves with pistols. When the Germans began to clear the ghetto in April 1943, they were met with armed resistance. In retaliation, they burned the ghetto down building by building. By mid-May, the ghetto had gone: 56,000 Jews had been killed or deported to death camps, 15,000 escaped to join the Polish resistance. Resistance in other Polish ghettos was similarly crushed and the ghettos cleared of all Jews.

1939–1943

Sept 1939–Sept 1941 "T4" programme kills 70,000 Germans.

Oct 1939 First Jewish ghetto created in Piotrkow, Poland.

Nov 1940 Warsaw ghetto established.

Jan–June 1941 13,000 Jews die of starvation in Warsaw ghetto; 5,000 in Lodz.

Feb Any Pole selling food to a Jew outside the Warsaw ghetto now automatically sentenced to three months hard labour; bread ration inside the ghetto reduced to 85 grammes a day.

Feb–May Three new ghettos established in Krakow, Kielce and Lublin; 40,000 German and Belgian Jews shipped into Warsaw ghetto.

April 1941 Any Jew caught leaving the Lodz ghetto now shot on sight.

June Ghettos set up in eastern Poland and USSR after German invasion of USSR.

Mar 1942 Germans begin to deport Jews from Polish ghettos to death camps; Jewish youth groups in Warsaw ghetto set up Jewish Combat Organisation to resist deportations.

Jan 1943 German police organising second major deportation from Warsaw ghetto are shot at by Jewish resistance fighters.

April Major German effort to clear Warsaw ghetto meets with armed uprising.

May Warsaw ghetto uprising ends with destruction of Warsaw's main synagogue.

The Final Solution

On 22 June 1941, 3.6 million German and allied troops crossed the Polish–Soviet frontier at the start of Operation Barbarossa, the invasion of the USSR. The invasion brought millions of Russian Jews under Nazi rule.

The Wannsee Conference

On 20 January 1942, Reinhard Heydrich, head of the Gestapo, summoned 14 leading Nazis to a villa on the shores of Lake Wanssee in Berlin. The meeting organised the "coming Final Solution of the Jewish question", that is the extermination of all Jews in Europe.

The conference drew up two lists of Jews: an A list of Jews living under direct Nazi control and a B list of those living in pro-Nazi independent states such as Slovakia and Romania or in Nazi enemy states such as Britain. The total came to more than 11 million. The meeting agreed that all Jews were eventually to be transported to the east to work themselves to death or be killed in camps. From now on, the final solution was the major priority of the Nazi war machine.

Preparing the Way

As German troops swept into Russia, Einsatzgruppen units shot as many Jews and communists as they could find. At least one million Jews were killed in the three Baltic states of Estonia, Latvia and Lithuania alone. However, it soon became clear that the use of murder squads and ghettos was not enough to clear the occupied areas of all Jews. A more efficient, "final solution" would be needed.

> ❝*In the course of the practical extension of the Final Solution, Europe will be combed through from west to east [of all Jews].*❞
>
> *Minutes of the Wannsee Conference, 20 January 1942*

At first the Nazis used mobile gas vans, in which victims were sealed inside and poisoned by exhaust fumes. When the victims were dead, the van was driven to a quiet place and the bodies were tipped out and burned or buried in mass graves. Although effective, the vans could not kill on a large scale. For that to happen, death camps would have to be built.

Death Camps

The first such camp was opened in December 1941 at Chelmno in Poland, followed by Belzec, Sobibor and Treblinka. All four were part of a campaign, known as *Aktion Reinhard*, to kill all Jews in the General Government or occupied part of Poland. A fifth death camp at Auschwitz was constructed next to an existing labour camp (see pages 22–23). Unlike the labour and concentration camps, these death camps had one aim: to kill Jews and others within a few hours of their arrival.

Each camp contained large gas chambers fed by exhaust fumes from diesel engines capable of killing thousands at a time. Jews stripped off their clothes and entered the gas chambers. Once they were sealed inside, the gas was turned on and death came within minutes. Fellow Jews then retrieved the bodies and burned them in crematoria.

Resistance

The scale of killing in death camps was immense. By the time they closed in 1943, 1.6 million Jews and thousands of Roma and others had been killed. Resistance, however, was common and revolts broke out in Treblinka and at Sobibor. Those who escaped took up arms as partisans. In total, some 30,000 partisans fought the Nazis in eastern Europe.

Women prisoners, heads shaved, stand before the camera at Auschwitz.

1941–1943

June 1941 Operation Barbarossa: German, Finnish, Italian, Romanian and Hungarian troops invade USSR.

Oct First mass transport of 22,000 Jews from Germany to the Polish ghettos, or to Riga or Minsk in Russia, where they were shot.

Nov 1,200 Jews gassed at Buchenwald concentration camp in first such experiment.

Dec First death camp opens at Chelmno near Lodz; 13,000 Jews gassed by Feb 1942.

Jan 1942 Nazi conference at Wannsee plans "final solution".

Mar New death camps open at Belzec and Sobibor, followed in June by Treblinka, all in occupied Poland.

May First gassings occur at new camp of Auschwitz.

Sept 1943 13 Jewish slave labourers in Treblinka kill their SS guard, steal his uniform and walk out of the camp to freedom.

Oct Major revolt in Sobibor leads to mass break-out of 600 Jews, 300 join Soviet partisan units; only 64 survive the war.

Dec All four camps destroyed in order to hide the evidence.

Auschwitz

One name sums up all the horrors of the Holocaust: Auschwitz. It was here that more than one million Jews and others met their deaths.

Why Did the Allies not Bomb Auschwitz?

Evidence of the extermination of the Jews in Europe was clear after 1942. Detailed information about Auschwitz itself was known from two Slovakian Jews who had escaped the camp in spring 1944. Indeed, a US Mosquito plane photographed the entire camp in August 1944, but the photo-interpreters were only interested in the I.G. Farben chemical plant and did not look at the nearby death camp.

The Allies decided that the best way to save the Jews was to defeat the Nazis. The practical difficulties of flying from southern Italy – the nearest Allied airbase – 2,000 kilometres across Europe to drop bombs on a gas chamber no bigger than a tennis court, without killing thousands of Jews, were just too great.

The Camp Opens

On 26 March 1942 a train took 2,000 Slovakian Jews to Auschwitz camp in southern Poland. The next day, another train left Paris loaded with 1,112 foreign-born Jews heading for the same destination. The death factory at Auschwitz was now in operation.

Auschwitz was in fact not a single camp, but three separate camps and at least 36 sub-camps spread out around the Polish town. The original camp, Auschwitz I, housed prisoners of war, homosexuals, Roma and political opponents.

Auschwitz–Birkenau (Auschwitz II) was by far the biggest of the three camps. It consisted of 250 barracks with about 100 support buildings and four vast crematoria. Each of these contained an undressing room, a gas chamber capable of killing 2,000 people at a time, and a set of ovens working day and night to burn the bodies.

Gateway to hell – the entrance to Auschwitz. Along these railway lines passed trains carrying hundreds of thousands to their deaths.

Auschwitz Monowitz (Auschwitz III) was a labour camp next door to the vast I.G. Farben petrochemical plant, built and run by slave labour to produce supplies for the German war effort.

A staff of more than 7,000 – administrators, guards, doctors and others, including many women – worked at the three camps.

The Killing Machine

Auschwitz was the largest single camp in the Nazi slave-labour system, processing more than 400,000 prisoners in over four years. It was also the biggest of the death camps.

Jews were brought by rail in cattle wagons from across Nazi-occupied Europe – from France and Holland in the west, from Italy, Greece and the Balkans in the south, and from the Baltic states and Russia in the east. Once off the trains, the SS guards separated "unfit" women, children, the old and the ill and sent them to the left, straight to the gas chambers. The women and men who remained were sent to the right, where they were tattooed with a number and sent to work in the labour camp.

In total, more than one million Jews, 70,000 Poles, 23,000 Roma, 15,000 Soviet prisoners of war, and many thousands of others died in Auschwitz. The reason we know so much about the camp is because when the Red Army liberated it in January 1945, the Germans did not have time to destroy all the buildings or kill its remaining inmates. Those who survived Auschwitz bore witness to its appalling history.

1940–1945

June 1940 Auschwitz I concentration camp opens to house Polish political prisoners.

Aug 1941 First experiments on Soviet prisoners in Auschwitz I using pellets of Zyklon B hydrogen-cyanide gas, originally a commercial pesticide used to kill vermin and made commercially by the chemical works next door.

Oct Construction begins of Auschwitz-Birkenau.

Mar 1942 First Jews, from Slovakia and France, taken to Auschwitz-Birkenau.

Mar–June Four new crematoria built at Auschwitz-Birkenau.

May First gassings using Zyklon B occur at Auschwitz-Birkenau.

Dec Nazis order all German gypsies to be taken to Auschwitz.

May 1944 First transport of Hungarian Jews to Auschwitz: 437,000 deported by July.

mid-1944 6,000 people a day killed in Auschwitz.

23 Aug US Mosquito reconnaissance aircraft photographs Auschwitz.

13 Sept American B-24 bombers destroy the chemical plant but miss death camp.

Jan 1945 Nazis blow up the crematoria at Auschwitz-Birkenau to hide evidence of their killings from advancing Soviet Red Army; 60,000 prisoners sent on "death march" towards Germany.

27 Jan Auschwitz liberated by Red Army; 7,650 prisoners found alive in the death camp, 200,000 more who had passed through the camp between 1940–45 also survived.

❝ *There were people in striped uniforms, shaven heads. It looked like an actual madhouse.* ❞

Esther Brunstein, Auschwitz survivor

Collaboration and Rescue

Today the Holocaust is seen as such a terrible event that it is almost impossible to understand how anyone could have supported it or helped it to happen. Yet many people collaborated in this tragedy. Others helped those caught up in it to escape.

1937–1945

1937 Pope Pius XI condemns Nazi racial ideas but not their anti-Jewish laws.

July–Aug 1941 Croatia begins to kill its Jews in six local concentration camps.

Oct 1941 Germans stop legal Jewish emigration because of war conditions.

July 1942 Germans arrest thousands of Dutch Jews and transport first 6,000 to Auschwitz; Frank family goes into hiding in Amsterdam.

Dec Pope Pius XII refuses to join Allied governments in condemning Nazi atrocities as he believes the numbers involved were exaggerated for propaganda purposes.

Sept 1943 Danish sailors and fishermen carry 7,906 Danish Jews to safety in Sweden.

Oct Pope Pius XII refuses to condemn deportation of 1,000 Jews from Rome to Auschwitz.

June 1944 Pope Pius XII makes his first appeal since start of Holocaust to Hungarian government to stop deportation of Jews to Auschwitz.

July–Oct Swedish diplomat Raoul Wallenberg saves thousands of Hungarian Jews by giving them food, shelter and Swedish passports.

Aug Frank family betrayed and sent to Auschwitz.

Mar 1945 Anne Frank dies in Bergen-Belsen.

Collaboration

The Holocaust was started by members of the Nazi Party, led by Adolf Hitler, but many other people soon became involved. In the countries Germany directly controlled, such as Poland, anti-Jewish measures were ordered by the German *Reichskommissars* (governors) and carried out by their officers on a massive scale. In semi-independent countries, however, the picture was more mixed: the government of Vichy France deported foreign-born Jews but refused to deport French Jews, Croatia and Romania killed large numbers of Jews, while Finland refused to co-operate at all. Denmark secretly shipped all its Jews over to neutral Sweden to save them from certain death, helped by a German diplomat, Georg Ferdinand Duckwitz, who planned the rescue with the Swedish government.

Involvement

Across Germany, many different people were involved in carrying out the Holocaust. Some, like the SS guards at Auschwitz and the other camps, were actively involved in the killings, but what about the train drivers who drove the trains full of Jews across Europe to the camps, or the signalmen who changed the points and gave the all-clear for the trains to run? Were they collaborating in murder, or just doing their jobs?

The Frank family hid for two years in the attic above an office. The secret entrance was hidden behind a bookcase.

Silent Support

Although Pope Pius XII refused to speak out against the Holocaust, individual nuns and priests hid Jewish children in convents and orphanages. In Italy, many adult Jews were housed in churches and monasteries disguised as monks and nuns. Individual Protestant priests also helped the Jews, but in general the Christian churches did little to prevent or condemn the Holocaust.

Rescue

Many Germans and other Europeans helped Jews by hiding them in their houses or passing them off as their own family – about 200,000 Jews survived in this way. In France, families took in Jews or helped them escape to neutral Spain or Switzerland: more than 200,000 out of a total of 300,000 French Jews survived the war.

Oskar Schindler, a German industrialist and member of the Nazi Party, saved 1,200 Jewish employees by saying they were "essential workers" in the German war effort and must not be taken to the death camps. His story later became a successful Hollywood film.

Anne Frank

Anne Frank was born in Germany, but moved with her family to Amsterdam in the Netherlands when the Nazis came to power in 1933.

After the Nazis occupied the Netherlands in 1940, the Franks went into hiding because they were Jewish and feared being sent to a concentration camp. In July 1942 they all hid in a secret room above Anne's father's office, surviving on food smuggled to them, until they were betrayed in August 1944 and sent to Auschwitz.

Anne and her sister were then sent to Bergen–Belsen camp, where they died. Anne's story is important because she left a diary that tells about her life in hiding. It is also important because, like many Jews, the Franks were betrayed by those who could have helped them.

Liberation

In 1944, the Allied armies began to liberate the death camps and bring the Holocaust to an end. Many people could not believe what they saw in the camps, while others have never forgotten it.

Surviving the Holocaust

About 300,000 Jews survived the camps and death marches, the biggest number, 60,000, in Bergen-Belsen.

Another 1.6 million European Jews survived Hitler's attempts to kill them. In Germany, 330,000 Jews escaped death, while 225,000 Polish Jews survived, many by escaping to Soviet Central Asia in 1939–40. The 50,000 Jews of Bulgaria were saved because the Bulgarian people refused to deport them, while 430,000 Romanian Jews were saved when the country changed sides in the war in August 1944; 300,000 Hungarian Jews also escaped death because their country was liberated by the Red Army before the SS could deport them.

More than 20,000 French, Dutch and Belgian Jews found safety in neutral Switzerland, Spain and Portugal.

The End in Sight

After the invasion of France in June 1944, the Allied armies began to close in on Nazi Germany – the American and British armies from the west, the Soviet Red Army from the east. The end of the war in Europe – and the end of Nazi tyranny – was in sight.

News about the Holocaust had circulated throughout the world from late 1941, but nobody had any real idea about conditions inside the camps.

Real Evidence

The first camp to be entered was Majdanek in eastern Poland in July 1944. The Soviets were appalled by what they found: human bodies piled up next to the barbed wire fences, seven large gas chambers and a massive crematorium. War correspondents recorded the scene and published their reports and photographs, the first real evidence the general public had of the Holocaust.

But here, as elsewhere at first, the Soviets found only ruins. As the Red Army advanced, the Germans destroyed the evidence by blowing up the camps and sending their inmates on lengthy "death marches" towards Germany. Thousands died on route. At Majdanek, 1,200 Jews had been evacuated only the day before. Yet extraordinarily, the Germans continued to kill Jews in huge numbers wherever possible. As the eastern-most camps were liberated in Poland, Jews continued to be transported to their deaths in German camps such as Dachau and Buchenwald.

Survivors Remain

On 27 January 1945 the Soviets entered Auschwitz. Here, unlike elsewhere, they found some survivors – just 7,650 people amid the piles of bodies; 98,000 Jews had been evacuated from the camp since late November and taken on open railway wagons through the bitter winter to camps in Germany itself. Most died on the journey.

In the west, British troops entered Bergen-Belsen camp in northwest Germany on 15 April. Inside they found 60,000 survivors, barely alive. Those with any strength turned on their guards, killing seven; the remaining guards – including many women – were put to work burying the 10,000 bodies piled up in the camp. In southern Germany, the American generals Eisenhower, Bradley and Patton burst into tears when confronted with the corpses piled up in Ohrdruf camp, while American troops were so appalled by what they found at Dachau that they shot dead 122 SS guards on the spot.

1941–1945

late 1941 British intercept German secret Enigma messages concerning the Holocaust.

Mar 1942 Jewish press in Palestine first report massacres of Jews in Ukraine.

June British newspapers first report news of 700,000 Jews massacred in Poland.

Aug Gerhard Riegner of World Jewish Congress sends telegram to US government detailing "final solution"; US government refuses to publish it because it does not believe it to be true.

March 1943 Bulgarian parliament unanimously refuses German request to deport 50,000 Jews.

22 July 1944 1,200 Jews evacuated frrom Majdanek to Auschwitz.

23 July Red Army enters Majdanek, the first camp to be discovered.

Nov 50,000 Hungarian Jews marched by SS to Vienna; 10,000 die on route.

27 Jan 1945 Red Army liberates Auschwitz.

18 Feb 500 German Jews married to Christians sent to their deaths in Theresienstadt camp in Bohemia.

4 April US troops liberate Ohrdruf; 4,000 Jews killed there since January.

15 April British troops liberate Bergen-Belsen.

29 April US troops liberate Dachau.

5 May Americans liberate Mauthausen in Austria, last camp to be liberated; 30,000 Jews killed there since January.

5 May German surrender brings World War Two and the Holocaust to an end.

Bergen-Belsen was liberated by British troops in April 1945. SS guards and German civilians were forced to remove the bodies of dead inmates.

Never Again

At the end of World War Two in Europe in May 1945, the Holocaust came to an end. But its impact remained considerable, and it is now commemorated around the world every year.

The Yad Vashem memorial in Jersualem commemorates Jewish victims of the Holocaust.

The Genocide Continues

Although the Holocaust stopped in 1945, anti-Semitism did not. After the war, 200,000 Jews who had fled Poland returned from Russia and elsewhere with Polish government support.

Almost immediately, 1,000 Jews – including some who had survived Auschwitz – were killed in new pogroms, forcing 100,000 to leave the country again by mid-1947.

Other acts of genocide have also taken place against other groups. Two million people – one-third of the population – were killed for political reasons in Cambodia between 1975 and 1979, while 750,000 Hutus and moderate Tutsis were killed in Rwanda in 1994 by Tutsi extremists. The lessons of the Holocaust must be remembered every day.

Justice

The immediate task facing the Allies in Germany was to feed and care for the 300,000 camp survivors and bring them back to health. Thousands were too weak to survive: 5,000 died at Belsen in the week after liberation, 3,000 at Mauthausen. Of those who survived, almost all had left Europe by 1950: 72,000 to the USA, 16,000 to Canada, and 200,000 to the new state of Israel.

Their second task was to bring the Nazis to justice. An international military court in Nuremberg tried 21 leading Nazis, of whom 11 were sentenced to death. A further 5,000 lower-ranking Nazis were also convicted over the next four years, many in the countries where they had committed their crimes. Trials of Nazi war criminals continue to this day.

The Creation of Israel

After the war, many Jews renewed their call for their own homeland. Illegal immigration to Palestine began again, and Jewish radicals soon clashed with the occupying British authorities. The British handed the problem over to the United Nations, which agreed to partition Palestine to create Jewish and Arab states. On 15 May 1948 the new state of Israel was founded. Jews at last had their own country.

Eichmann and After

In the years immediately after the war, the Holocaust faded from memory. Many who had lived through it found it too painful to remember, while young Israelis, many from the Arab world, did not identify with their European elders. All this changed in 1960, when Adolf Eichmann – the man most responsible for the organisation of the Holocaust in Auschwitz and elsewhere after 1941 – was brought to trial.

His trial showed that there was indeed a plan to exterminate the Jews, and that people as ordinary as Eichmann had been responsible. "I sat at my desk and did my work," he said, but so too did many thousands of other people responsible for the deaths of millions.

After the trial, interest in the Holocaust grew. Museums were set up to record its history, while every year on 27 January – the anniversary of the liberation of Auschwitz – the world commemorates Holocaust Day and pledges that never again will such an appalling event occur.

> **❝ We are on the brink of the moment when this terrible event will change from memory to history. ❞**
>
> *Silvan Shalom, Israeli foreign minister, speaking at Auschwitz on the 60th anniversary of its liberation, 27 January 2005*

1945–2005

May 1945–May 1948 83,000 Jews shipped illegally to Palestine by Jewish organisations in defiance of British restrictions; British turn back many more.

July 1945 First Jewish camp-survivors conference held in St Ottlien camp, Munich; it calls for immediate establishment of a Jewish state in Palestine.

Aug 23 Allied nations agree to set up war crimes trials to bring Nazis to justice.

Nov–Sept 1946 Main war crimes trial held at Nuremberg, Germany; 12 other trials of 156 less-important German and Austrian war criminals end in 1947.

July 1946 41 Jews killed in pogrom in Kielce, Poland; 1,000 die by mid-1947.

Feb 1947 Britain hands decision over future of Palestine to UN.

July *Exodus* ship, carrying 4,500 camp survivors, is intercepted by British in Mediterranean and turned back to France; its passengers are then deported to Germany; affair creates international outrage and forces UN to act.

Nov UN agrees to divide Palestine into two independent states: Arab and Jewish.

14 May 1948 State of Israel founded and immediately fights for its life against Arab invaders.

July 1950 Israeli Law of Return proclaims: "Every Jew has the right to come to this country as an immigrant."

May 1960 Israeli secret agents capture Eichmann in Argentina and bring him back to Israel for trial.

May 1962 Eichmann found guilty and hanged for mass murder.

Jan 2005 World leaders and Holocaust survivors gather at Auschwitz to commemorate 60th anniversary of the liberation of the camp.

May 2005 Holocaust Memorial opens in Berlin, capital of Hitler's Nazi empire.

Glossary

Allies, the USA, USSR, Britain and others fighting Germany during World War Two.

Ally A country linked with another by treaty or friendship.

Anti-Semitism Prejudice against Jewish people.

Armed services The military forces of a nation, usually army, air force and navy.

Armistice An agreement between opposing sides to cease fire while a peace agreement is agreed.

Colony The region or country controlled by another country as part of an empire.

Communism Belief in a society that exists without different social classes and in which everyone is equal and all property is owned by the people.

Concentration camp A prison camp where Jews and others were held in captivity and worked to death.

Death camp Also called an extermination camp, where Jews and others were systematically killed, usually by poison gas.

Dictator A leader who takes complete control of a country and often rules by force.

Einsatzgruppen "Action groups": special murder squads of SS officers ordered to kill enemies of the state, notably Jews and communists in occupied Poland and Russia.

Empire A group of different nations and peoples, ruled by one nation and its emperor or king.

Final Solution *Endlösung* in German: the "final solution of the Jewish question" was the German phrase used to describe the extermination of all Jews in Europe.

Führer German word for "leader", a title taken by Hitler after 1934.

Genocide The deliberate destruction of a racial, religious, political or ethnic group.

Ghetto A poor part of a town or city where Jews were forced to live.

Hitler, Adolf (1889–1945) The leader of the German Nazi Party 1921–45, and ruler of Germany 1933–45.

Holocaust, the Deliberate attempt by Nazis to kill all Jews in Europe.

Labour camp A camp using slave labour, mostly Jews and prisoners of war, to produce materials for the German war effort.

Lebensraum German word meaning "living room", land in eastern Europe that Hitler wished to see inhabited by Germans.

Manifesto A public statement of political beliefs, policies and aims issued by a political party or leader.

Nazi Party Extreme political party led by Adolf Hitler that ruled Germany from 1933–45.

Neutral Describes a nation that refuses to take sides in a war and does not fight.

Partisan A member of armed resistance group fighting inside a country against an invading or occupying army.

Pogrom An organised massacre of a group of people, often Jews, within a society.

Red Army Army of the USSR.

SS, the *Schutzstaffel* or "protection squads", originally set up to protect senior members of the Nazi Party but later developed into the organisation responsible for the Einsatzgruppen and the death camps.

Treaty A formal agreement between two or more countries.

USSR Union of the Soviet Socialist Republics, or the Soviet Union, which existed from 1922–91; commonly known as Russia.

WEBSITES

www.holocaustmemorialday.gov.uk
The British government's official website marking Holocaust Day, with case studies on the resistance and life in the ghettos and camps.

www.ushmm.org
US Holocaust Memorial Museum website, with full details of the museum, and of the holocaust, the camps and recent acts of genocide.

www.auschwitz-muzeum.oswiecim.pl
The official Auschwitz website on the history of the camp and its status today as a museum.

www.aish.com/holocaust
Israeli website on the Holocaust, with a detailed history, discussion of the issues and personal memoirs.

www.library.yale.edu/testimonies
A collection of more than 4,200 videotaped interviews with witnesses and survivors of the Holocaust.

Index